There Is A Story Behind My Praise

By: Cassandra Wainright

Published by Purpose Publishing
1503 Main Street #168 ❧ Grandview, Missouri
www.purposepublishing.com

ISBN: 978-0-9858266-2-8

Cover design by: Thaddeus Jordan
Editing by: Brenda Cotton
Photography by: Calvon Wainright of Double XPosure
Photography

Printed in the United States of America

This book is available at quantity discounts for bulk
purchases. Inquiries may be addressed to:

Pastor Cassandra Wainright
11200 E. 75th Terrace
Raytown, MO 64138
Church: 816-497-4886
Cell: 816-716-3473
Email: Sandywainright@aol.com

Dedication

I dedicate this book to those who know me best. Those whom have seen me in the best of times and in the worst of times:

My Loving Husband: Calvin Carzell Wainright
My Mother: Prophetess & Evangelist Earlene Davis
My Siblings: Gloria Shareef, Leon Davis, Jr., Karla Jackson, Vickie Givens, Dana White, Myrcon Davis and Eric "Larond" Davis (In Memoriam)

My Children: Kiana D'Nai Boyington and Stephaun Donte' Jackson.

My Children added to me by GOD: Tina Shenice Johnson, Ishmail Carzell Wainright and Amaad Carzell Wainright.

To The Heaven Sent Outreach Ministries Church Family who has loved, interceded for and supported the call that God has on my life.

Finally, to my heart: My Grandchild, Aa'Laiza Anais Cole, who has brought me so much joy and the one who shall carry my legacy forward!!

> *"For thus saith the Lord, that after seventy years be accomplished at Babylon, I will visit you, and perform My good Word toward you, in causing you to return to this place. For I know the thoughts that I think toward you, saith the Lord, thoughts of peace, and not of evil, to give you an expected end. Then shall ye call upon Me, and ye shall go and pray unto Me, and I will hearken unto you. And ye shall seek Me, and find Me, when ye shall search for Me with all your heart!"*
> **Jeremiah 29: 10-14**

A Special Dedication

This book is dedicated in loving memory of my Aunt (my Mom's baby Sister),

Jessie Ruth ("Harania") Scott,

who throughout both my childhood and adult life shared my struggles and became my very best friend and confidant as she tirelessly encouraged me in the midst of my storms.

Aunt Harania…"And I Shall Always Love You!"

Acknowledgements

Let me first and foremost begin by saying that, I give reverence, honor and great appreciation to Almighty God, my Motivator and my Sustainer, for His awesome gifting in my life. Through the richness of His love and the truth of His Word, I can totally declare that He who hath begun a good work in you (me) shall continue to perform it until the day of Jesus Christ.

To Bishop Eric D. Morrison, my Father in the Gospel, who prophesied and spoke a Rhema Word in my life in August, 2006 by instructing me ~ by the Spirit and unction of the Lord ~ to begin to write my book. Bishop, I heard; received and obeyed! F-I-N-A-L-L-Y!

To my Husband, Partner & Friend, Pastor Calvin C. Wainright – Thank you so much for the priceless treasure of your love and support of everything God has given me to do. Thank you for being the best thing on this earth that could have ever happened to me. I thank you for your unconditional love and undying support. You are truly my gift from God!

To my "sister" and special friend, LaTanya Cooper…you and I have said for years that we would write a book one day. Okay Sister, here's mine! Let's get started on yours!

To Ms. Grace LaJoy Henderson, who hosted a free "Writers Breakthrough Workshop" in May, 2007 right at the time when God was seriously dealing with me concerning starting this project. Your personal testimony, endurance and instruction gave me the boldness to declare "if she can do it, I can, too!"

To Ms. Adele Foster, who mentored and coached Grace LaJoy Henderson through the publishing process. To know that you saw talent and you assisted someone else in reaching their full potential, has blessed me more than you will ever know.

To "**Minister**" **Angel Collins-Wilson** who prophetically spoke a word in prayer to me in November, 2009 that I would write a book that would give Glory and honor to God.

To **Dr. Margaret C. Wright** who introduced her book "Training The Prophet" to our ministry in November, 2008 and told my daughter to tell me that whenever I was ready to write my book, she would refer me to her publisher. Your book inspired me to believe I could, too! And I will never forget the Word of prophecy you declared in my life years ago. Though I did not understand it then, God has made it crystal clear to me now. You told me that God said "…whatever I wanted to do, He would give me the Grace to do it!" Thank you, Dr. Wright, for such a Rhema Word!

To **Pastor Donald R. Akers**- Thank you for being my faithful friend! Thank you for your support of this book and for "cheerleading" me through this process. I am forever grateful to GOD for such a friend as you!

To **Michelle Gines of Purpose Publishing** who entered my life at an awesome God moment! Thank you for accepting this project and making it come alive! Thank you for your encouragement; your expertise; your love for God and the things of God; your inspiration and guidance; and for literally carrying me through this entire publishing process. You were ordained for me for such as time as this!!!

To **Brenda Cotton, Editor of Purpose Publishing**- Oh my God! At our very first encounter, you spoke such a Rhema Word to me; prophetically pouring into my life. Thank you for affirming this project and helping me see its potential to bless the people of God. Thank you for your partnership in Purpose Publishing and for being an overwhelming blessing in my life and ministry!

To my family, you have been such an integral part of my life-long journey. You have shared each story that has been included in this book. You have loved me. You have supported me. You have prayed for me and have always stood beside me. I am grateful that God placed me with such a wonderful, loving and accepting family as you!

And finally, to my mother, Prophetess & Evangelist Earlene Davis- Thank you for granting me permission to share this part of my life. I know that for me to tell my story means that I also tell a portion of yours. You have become my very closest friend; my confidante; my intercessor and my support! Mom, I'm grateful for the seasons God has triumphantly brought us through!

What others are saying about "There Is A Story Behind My Praise."

Who should read this book? EVERYONE!
Who WILL be blessed by this book? EVERYONE!
This book is especially for those that have EVER questioned the plan for their life; those that have been down to NOTHING and watched our incredible God raise them up to SOMETHING! This book is for you.
-*Minister Patrice Perkins*

The readers will benefit from the transparency of her testimony. The fact that there is a woman speaking on the topic of promiscuity brings to the forefront a hidden and unspoken truth that is prevalent in many women.
-*Bishop Eric D. Morrison*
Pastor, Kingdom Word Ministries

In her story, Pastor Wainright reveals the raw emotions and convoluted thinking that accompanies forbidden sex, betrayal and deception. Her story is one that will keep you hanging on every page.
-*Pastor Donald R. Akers,*
Lift HIM Up Ministries Family Worship Center

Foreword

To God be the Glory!! As you read this book, I pray you will rejoice and think about all of God's goodness to you. Do as I have done…**"let all bitterness, indignation, wrath, resentment, quarreling and slander be banished from you."** (Ephesians 4:31 Amplified Version)

I am the proud mother of the young lady whom God has called to write this book. It is a book that will bless anyone who has been hurt as a result of the terrible injustices that have been done to them, at any given age. Just the thought of someone hurting a child, would make anyone cry. I thank God that this book is a testament that there is forgiveness, restoration and healing for anyone that calls upon the Name of the Lord.

With the writing of this book, my daughter intimately shares her life story. I believe it has been another vehicle that God is using to erase all of the hurt and unforgiveness completely from her mind and heart. As you read her story, He will do the same for you.

I will be praying on behalf of everyone who will read, "There Is A Story Behind My Praise" and believing God will do just what He said He would do. **"Therefore, if anyone is in Christ, he is a new creation; the old has gone; the new has come!"** (II Corinthians 5:17 NIV) Let it go! Let it go! God has forgiven all of our sins…whatever they may have been!

Remember, the Word of God says, **"And we know that ALL things work together for good to them that love God, to them who are the called according to His purpose**_!"_ (Romans 8:28 KJV) As you see, my daughter has become a Pastor of "The Sent", along with her husband. She has a son and daughter, grandchildren; and a Church Family that loves her very much, as well as her own biological family. Pastor Sandy had to recall God's Word that says, _"_**for I am confident of this very thing, that He who began a good work in you will**

perfect it until the day of Christ Jesus." (Philippians 1:6 NASB) He is able to do all things through you!

As you read this book, let love abide in your heart and remember this young lady is one of God's chosen vessels, called to help countless others. There is forgiveness and release for those who carry heavy burdens – whatever they may be. No, you may not have had the same experiences that my daughter had, but nonetheless, you have experienced your share of pain and heartache.

The things my daughter is sharing in her book were meant to destroy her. The things that happened to her as a child could have literally destroyed our family. Satan's plan was to abort God's purpose for us. The bitterness, mistrust and resentment my daughter felt, could have crushed her. I thank God for restoration, deliverance, healing and wholeness! I thank God for allowing my daughter to share her story!

The mandate of this book is discovered in Luke 4:18-19 (CEV) when Jesus said, "**The Lord's Spirit has come to Me, because He has chosen Me to tell the good news to the poor. The Lord has sent Me to announce freedom for prisoners; to give sight to the blind; to free everyone who suffers, and to say, this is the year the Lord has chosen!**"

The Spirit of the Lord has breathed upon Pastor Sandy, and she is sharing the good news and by reading her book, you, too, can become free!

With Much Love, Her Mother,

Ms. Earlene Davis, Prophetess & Evangelist

Table Of Contents

Introduction

I was riding in my car one day and I heard this little song come on the radio. I began to cry uncontrollably as I related to the passion and the fervor of Ms. Carolyn Traylor ministering, "There Is A Story Behind My Praise". So many memories came to mind in the midst of my tears. It's been a long and unique journey, but I'm still here to talk about it…

At the time that this writing began, I was 51 years-old. For years, I had a dream of writing a book of my life, but lacked direction and guidance on getting started and honestly, felt that it would remain an unfulfilled dream because I didn't have the confidence to believe I could really do it.

God had already given me titles for several publications and I would always write them down somewhere. Always saying to myself…"maybe someday". I knew I had a story to tell and even in the midst of sharing my personal testimonies in ministry, God made it ever so plain that everything I had experienced in life was for purpose and that it would serve to bless countless others.

There were times in my life that I felt like I was the only one going through this; that I was the only one these things were happening to. As I matured, I discovered that I was not alone in my struggles. Others had experienced the same kind of hurt, disappointment, rejection and abuse but were keeping those memories of a painful past hidden away in dark closets of their souls. No one wants to have to relive days of anguish, despair, betrayal and hurt but I found my healing and deliverance in the midst of me sharing my story. I can rejoice now and I am totally free to give God all the Glory, but I want – no, I need – for others to know that *"There Is A Story Behind My Praise!"*

So for those who have lived your lives with "bottled up" emotions, this book is for YOU! For those who find it difficult or impossible to see how any good thing can come out of the hell you have lived through, this book is for YOU! For those who are living through pain, betrayal, heartbreak and heartache, this book is for YOU! For those who wish to encourage someone else you know, this book is for YOU! To every child, teenager, young adult, this book will reveal the extent of a parent's unconditional love. Like me, everything may not have gone the way you would have planned it, but just keep living! God will reveal Himself to you as He writes your story. To every mother with the God-given responsibility to raise, protect and nurture your children, this book is for YOU!

Take this literary journey with me. Your outcome can be even greater than mine. I thank God that He allowed me to live long enough to declare to satan himself as Joseph said in Genesis 50:19-20 *"...***but as for you, ye thought evil against me; but God meant it unto good, to bring to pass, as it is this day, to save much people alive."**

I know all too well that, so many of us go about our day to day lives, holding on to 'stuff' that we can't seem to shake loose! We go – day in and day out – functioning, but never fully blossoming. It's because of the tons of baggage we carry; the weights that keep us down; the oppression that satan fights to not let go of over our lives – yet, we serve a God that has declared that He alone knows the plans that He has for you.

No, it may not be the same story as mine, but it is a story nonetheless! No, it may not be the same struggles as mine, but you've fought all your life just trying to break free! No, you didn't lose your mind; you didn't commit suicide – you have lived to tell your story! After reading this book, it is my prayer that you won't let obstacles from your past continue to bombard you.

This book is written to offer hope and encouragement in the midst of hard and desolate times. Don't sit and let the enemy convince you that you need to stay ashamed of your past. We serve an awesome Savior who is the God that healeth thee! So no matter how long it's been or how long you have held it in, today is your time to be set free. It happened...but it's over! And you, too, have ***a story behind your praise!***

Chapter 1:
It Had To Begin Somewhere

"Then the word of the Lord came unto me, saying,
Before I formed thee in the belly I knew thee;
And before thou camest forth out of the womb
I sanctified thee, And I ordained thee a prophet unto
the nations." **Jeremiah 1:4-5**

In April, 2007, I, along with others attended a Pastoral Appreciation Service at Memorial Missionary Baptist Church. During that service, a lady in the choir began to minister a song that I've heard on many occasions. But at this time; on this date, the Holy Spirit immediately spoke and said "Sandy, that is the name of your book". She was singing the words to this song:

"There Is A Story Behind My Praise
That's why my hands, I continue to raise
I'm gonna praise Him for the rest of my days cause
There's A Story Behind My Praise!"

It was on that particular Sunday, that this song took on a different meaning and gave new revelation such as I have not known. It was as if a "clean sweep" went through my mind to many, many years back. A snapshot of difficult and trying moments vividly came before me and in each "mental picture", God was always there!

Sitting in the church listening to this woman (thank you, Minister Calandra Sumpter) powerfully minister this song, God said to me "This is what it was all about! This is the reason you had to go through so!" Oh, did my heart not burn with fire!

Within this book, I will attempt to share some chapters from my life's story. Hopefully, you'll see why **"there is a story behind my *praise*!"**

My start – my beginning, as we understand life, was in 1956. That is when I made my debut into the world. Of course, I don't have any recollection of anything in those infant/toddler years. So I guess you could say life for me was pretty 'peachy'.

However, at age 5, life began to become crystal clear for me. My parents had divorced and at this time, my mom had been remarried. From all appearances, things were well in our home. We attended church as a family. Our mom was the disciplinarian. She brought our family together each and every week for family prayer time. We would sing, read scriptures and pray. Our mom was usually the last to pray and for me and my two siblings (at that time), her prayers seem to have lasted forever. Oftentimes, she would find us knelt down on our knees slumped over on the couch and falling asleep as she prayed. Our stepfather was a good man; excellent provider; laid back with a sense of humor. We grew to respect him because he chose to assume the role of husband and father for a divorced woman with three young daughters.

I was the middle daughter at that time; the second eldest. My sisters and I dressed well. We lived as my husband says "in the high rise" apartments like the Jefferson's a couple blocks away from the housing projects. Our friends were always impressed by our way of living – three meals a day eaten and shared as a family sitting at the table together; and having to come in from outside when the street lights came on. To us, life was good!

Time for Reflections

Take a few moments to share your beginning. Where did it all begin for you?

_____

_____

_____

_____

_____

_____

_____

_____

_____

_____

_____

_____

_____

_____

_____

_____

_____

Chapter 2:
So When Did the
Pain Begin?

"Beloved, think it not strange concerning the fiery trial which is to try you, As though some strange thing happened unto you..."
I Peter 4:12

For me, age 5 was a turning point in my life. Though there are many very vivid memories from that period of my life, I am grateful that it would seem that God has completely erased some others.

I recall times that my mom would head to church for mid-week meetings. Though we all attended church as a family, there were some infrequent times that mom would leave us home with our dad (stepdad).

Note: You will note that from this point on, I will refer to our stepfather only as Dad or Daddy. My sisters didn't grow up differentiating our fathers. From birth, we were with our natural father, Frank Scott Emery, and we loved him deeply. As sisters, during our early years of life, we decided that we would not refer to our stepdad as Mr. Leon nor call him step-daddy. We bestowed upon him, Leon Davis, Sr., the same title (and honor) as we had with Frank Emery. Therefore, we called him Daddy too!

There were some evenings that we would stay home with Daddy while Mom attended church. It's strange as I think about it, even now, but for some reason, I don't remember my other two sisters being home with me. I only remember me and Daddy (Leon). There were times that I recall him fondling me and having me fondle him. I can't honestly tell you how it even began. I just remember the times he would give me money and say "don't tell your mama or anybody...remember this is our little secret!" That's all I can remember. No more and no less! I know there was more than one time that it happened. I don't remember how often nor how long- I just know it happened. I can't even remember when it stopped. I just know it did. I have no recollection of him actually penetrating me sexually but always fondling with me and even more vividly, having me fondle him.

This is what I actually have to thank God for. As devastating as some things can be, I am so very grateful that He has literally erased some of these memories from my mind. I was young, naïve and innocent. As I just stated, I don't even recall Daddy actually penetrating me or having sex with me. I don't know if that ever actually happened. What I do remember was that I was only 5 years-old!! Look at your 5 year-old child; look at your 5 year-old niece or grandchild! I was only 5 years old!

Time for Reflections

Be honest. How many people in your family have suffered abuse at the hands of a family member, close friend or acquaintance?

_____

_____

_____

_____

_____

_____

Identify the single greatest lesson you have learned from reading this particular chapter.

_____

_____

_____

_____

_____

_____

_____

Time for Reflections

What are the warning signs of abuse and how can you protect your loved ones from becoming a victim?

_____

_____

_____

_____

_____

_____

What teachable moments can you use with children and teens to help them identify an abuser and what they should do in a dangerous situation – no matter who it is?

_____

_____

_____

_____

_____

_____

_____

Time for Reflections

What scripture passage can you identify that would be able to speak to you in a situation as this?

_____

_____

_____

_____

_____

_____

Footnote:

For Men and Women everywhere, allow me to share my heart with you! We all have been created for God's divine purpose and we are awesome vessels in the Hands of God.

To every parent, step-parent; teacher, uncle, mentor, coach, Pastor; counselor; friend…God didn't position you in the life of a child or young teen to prey on them and strip them of their youth and their innocence! Know that you will stand before our Sovereign God to answer for attempting to rob the future of one of His precious children.

Chapter 3:
It's All A Façade!

"For if any be a hearer of the word, and not a doer, He is like unto a man beholding his natural face in a glass: For he beholdeth himself, and goeth his way, and straightway forgetteth what manner of man he was." James 1:23-24

Fast-forward a few years... I don't know how long the sexual abuse lasted. I don't remember how many years passed. I only remember my mom, my siblings and I visiting over to my grandparents' house one evening. I was outside talking with my uncle for some reason. I don't remember if anyone else was with us or if we were outside alone. I can't really imagine that because I didn't want to be alone with any other man. The things that happened with my father and me made me fearful of being around other men - relatives or not.

For some reason (and as I look back on it now), I know it was just the divine work of God, that I told my uncle about what my dad had been doing to me. I don't recall if my uncle told my mom that same night or not. I just knew that once my mom was told, ALL hell broke out!

Life for my family was never the same after that. Our home was never the same! I could go to school or church or anywhere else and life for our family looked good from the outside looking in. I made good grades at school, developed close friendships; had an excellent rapport with teachers and adults at school and at church. But at home – well, that was a totally different story.

To be home meant years of being accused of somehow all of this being my fault. Like I said before, I can't tell you when Daddy stopped – I just know he did. It could have very well been once my uncle told my mom...I just can't remember. Home for me was hell! I loved going to school, church or anywhere else just to escape the hell I was living in.

After my mom found out, Daddy and I experienced years of verbal abuse from my mom. She would lash out weekly (seemed like daily) accusations of him still 'messing' with me and me allowing him to do it. She accused me as if I intentionally allowed this to happen and that somehow I was deriving great pleasure seeing what this was doing to her.

I was miserable! My mom was miserable! My dad was miserable! My siblings were miserable! Our home was miserable! This whole thing became public knowledge to my grandparents, aunts, uncles, etc. I hated to go around any of them because I knew everybody knew. Mom didn't care where she was when she lashed out! She didn't care who was around to hear it. If it was at home, anyone who was there heard her go off on me or/and Daddy. We could be at the dinner table and she would accuse us of looking at each other! We could all be in the house together, and she would accuse me or him of going into one room, trying to sneak and meet up with each other. I'm not exaggerating when I tell you that our lives (not just mine) was a living HELL!

There were countless times when I would go to the basement room my sisters and I shared. I would lie on my bed and just cry myself sick. No comfort from my mom...she was too mad. No comfort from my dad...he would then be accused again. Only my oldest sister, Gloria, would come down to try to comfort me, but even she couldn't ease my pain. This went on for years – from elementary to middle school. I thought I would literally lose my mind. You can't imagine how often I asked God to just let me die. That would be the only way I would ever find relief.

We appeared to be the ideal blended family. A dad with an excellent job. A stay-at-home mom, caring for her family. Children who dressed well; ate well; our entire family going to church each and every Sunday. We were enjoying life - if you were on the outside looking in. Daddy served as a deacon in our church. We attended every service the church had. As youth, we were a part of the choir and every other youth group the church had. A family to be admired. A two-parent home that seemed to have it all together. The pastor didn't know...the church members didn't know...and of course, our father, Frank Emery, was never told. Who would have known...that it was all a façade?

Time for Reflections

Can you identify what the level of extreme pain that must have gone on in my family? Explain.

_____

_____

_____

_____

_____

_____

If you have ever been in a family situation that felt like a literal "hell", how did you distance yourself from it (whether mentally, emotionally or physically)?

_____

_____

_____

_____

_____

_____

Time for Reflections

A family in turmoil…what do you do?

_____

_____

_____

_____

_____

_____

If this is your story (or anything similar), how do you deal with what has happened?   How do you get past this traumatic experience?

_____

_____

_____

_____

_____

_____

_____

Time for Reflections

Can you identify a scripture passage that would be able to encourage you or others in a situation such as this?

_____

_____

_____

_____

_____

_____

_____

_____

_____

_____

_____

_____

_____

_____

Chapter 4:
Looking For Love In All The Wrong Places

"How is the faithful city become an harlot!"
Isaiah 1:21

Do you really know what it's like to feel unloved as a child? Can you imagine the pain that comes from being rejected?

So here goes that all too familiar story from us females, who did not have a true father figure in our homes. Most of us girls who now live in women's bodies, can attest to growing up without our daddy. For me, our real daddy was not in our home. We saw him when we needed something, or on special occasions. Though he was only a phone call away, the times we spent with 'Frank', was not a replacement for him being with us every day. So what did I do, girls? I looked for love in other places. (You know exactly where I'm going with this, don't you?)

Because of the molestation early in life, I became interested in boys at a young age. I remember calling "Greg" (a little white boy) in my kindergarten class, my first boyfriend. After that, all in elementary school – especially in the 4th and 5th grades, I became boy-crazy and enjoyed the time and attention they gave me one, right after the other. In junior high, my interest in boys continued. By high school, I could write a list of all the boyfriends I had. One in particular, became my first true love. As a freshman in high school, I fell for a high school dropout. My parents and grandparents *initially* couldn't stand him because he was considered a thug.

He hung out on Vine Street and everyone feared him and his friends. For some reason, I was drawn to him. I don't really remember just how we met, but at some point, he and his family became our next door neighbors. He was jealous…wouldn't let me talk to anyone, but there was something about him that I fell in love with and even now, I look at him as the angel God sent to look after me during my high school years. He was the one I lost my virginity to…for real. Remember, I told you I don't recall my dad ever actually penetrating me so I don't remember ever having sex before age 14. But this 17 or 18 year-old young man that I fell in love with, protected me. He protected me from girls who were jealous of me at school. He protected me from the girls he once dated that still wanted him and never liked me. I believe he understood my youth and even allowed me to date other boys at my school, until he felt I was getting too serious about them. Then, he would show up and run them out of my life. I was loving that! Here was a man who all I could see was someone taking care of me. He looked after me and made sure to protect not only me, but my family and friends as well. He saw me through my high school years, but still I searched for more…

After graduation, my life was busy with man after man. Some good; some not so good. (Aww, come on girls, you know we always let the good ones slip away! For some crazy reason, we are drawn to the 'no good' ones. Aww, that's you, too?) I partied; I clubbed; I had multiple sexual partners in my young life – all too numerous to name. That's why I preach untiringly to my own children because I remember how wild I was.

That search for love not only followed me through school and young adult life. It followed me in marriage. I was 21 when I first married a young man I knew in high school and dated after graduation. He was a good man; hard worker; came from a good family, but our marriage was a rocky one. At 21, I just wanted to be married. I wasn't ready to be married, but I just wanted to be someone's wife. I had moved out of my mom's home as soon as I graduated in mid-term of my senior year in high school, promising myself that I would never ever return. Oh, I need to go back for a minute. At some point (and again, I really don't remember when…sorry about that), my dad and I were at home together. I was older and had gone through so much mess with my mom, of course. One day out of nowhere, Daddy came and apologized to me. He told me he was sorry for all the things he had done to me. And he knew how much he had hurt me and my mom. He asked me to forgive him and you know what, I immediately did! I really think that I never hated him for what he did to me. I don't think I ever really had time. I spent so much time hating my mom for openly accusing me all those years and faulted her for making my life a living hell, that I never had time to resent my Daddy. He promised me that he would never touch me or approach me inappropriately and you know what, he never did. Did my mother believe that? Of course not! Even when I told her that Daddy apologized to me, she still kept the accusations going. Even though he probably apologized to her as well, she still hollered the accusations that whatever the relationship was – was continuing.

Now back to my first marriage – yes, you read it right… my first marriage. We were young and both had our own set of friends. He could hang with his friends but he never wanted me with mine. He had a car that he hardly allowed me to drive. He preferred taking me wherever I needed to go. That type of madness led to our separation and divorce. We began to experience numerous problems as a young couple and for me, enough was enough. We would separate and then reconcile, but the same things would occur so we eventually called it quits. We would argue about what church to attend on alternate Sundays. He was Methodist; I was Baptist. We would argue over which family we would spend Thanksgiving and Christmas with. Did we have premarital counseling? NOT! Did we really have an understanding of what sacrifices would be required in marriage? NOT!

After that failed relationship, I began to party a lot. I always loved to "two-step" (that's a dance ya'll!). Let me put a pen right here. Christian marriages or (let me rephrase this) two

Christians getting married or not...get counseling before marriage. No matter how young or old, I repeat, get counseling before marriage. No matter if it is your first marriage or fourth marriage, seek counseling. Just because you read the Bible, pray during the week and attend somebody's church, will not prevent marital differences and/or struggles. Seek out quality counseling with your Pastor or priest; even couples who have 'managed' to stay together in spite of. I know some marital experts will want to shoot me for this, but I even recommend counseling with someone whose marriage failed. Someone you trust – who has your happiness and well-being at heart – can be a truly great resource for discovering some pitfalls you can avoid in marriage. Just listening to how a failed marriage effected someone else you care about, can provide you the enlightenment and fortitude to persevere in the midst of struggles you are sure to encounter.

Oh! And while I am dodging bullets, let me insert this for those who don't already know...a marriage with quantity of years does not automatically equate to it being a quality marriage! From generations to generations, couples have stayed in a marriage for different reasons. Some for the sake of children having both parents in the home - only to discover that once children are grown and on their own, they had nothing else in common. Their married life revolved around caring for the children. Or let's see now, the couple that stays together because of finances. It would be too much of a financial burden for one or the other to call it quits and start all over again. The life of comfort has become a poor substitute for two people being together because of their love and commitment to each other. Finally (and quite sadly), some couples stay together (no matter how unhappy they are) because it's just plain convenient – and somehow, they can still do whatever they want with no conscious or moral conviction that they are dead wrong. I mean cheating on your spouse. Going home sleeping at night with the person you said "I Do" to and by day, sleeping with the person(s) you just 'do it' to! Sad to say, a lot of spouses have become so good at it, that they even stay out until late in the night or sometimes fail to come home at all, to spouses who put up with that madness.

Sorry – been there; done that! It doesn't work for me!

Am I against marriage? Absolutely not! Marriage is to symbolize the love relationship between Christ and His Bride (the church). As you read this, some of you might think that I am against marriage. Not so. But I am against bad marriages and I am against getting or staying married for the wrong reasons. Marriage was ordained to be between a man and a woman and is to reflect Christ's love for the church. He loves His "Bride" unconditionally and gave His life for "her". When two people can comprehend that 'mystery' and put God as the focal point of their lives, marriage is all worth it.

With all that said, let me get back to my story. Forgive me for digressing a little bit. After my first marriage failed, I began to party a lot. I would go out with the girls and enjoyed dancing with men who could really "two-step". I had started dating again and never had a problem with loneliness or being alone. Men were plentiful. I had no lack in that area. There was one guy who would always be at the parties I attended. Handsome as he could be. A real ladies' man and he knew it. He dressed good; looked good; danced good – a winning combination! Because of what I considered my success in having men…mind you, I was successful in having them. However, that statement says nothing about my ability to keep them. This one carried himself like he thought he was God's gift to women and he had no problem 'pulling' one or two or three on any given night. For me, I knew I had no problem with men wanting to 'pull' me, so we were tit for tat in that category (winking my eye). In all my life, I never had to approach any man. We weren't raised to approach or initiate any conversations with guys we had an interest in. We were taught that if a boy or man wanted you, let them do the pursuing. Mom instilled in us that "you don't chase men!!" I was intrigued by the smoothness of this one, though. I kept my eye on him while watching him connect with other females almost weekend, after weekend. He even dated one of my girlfriends at the time. That was fine by me because I was dating her cousin during that same time.

37

Much later, while we were all still in our party days, I saw him out one night. For the first time, we danced and my immediate thought was, "I need to show him something different than whatever he's been used to". Stupid...stupid...stupid! Well, we danced. He was an excellent dancer-extremely smooth. Oh, and did I mention he was handsome? Oh, and did I tell you he smelled good? We danced more than once together – danced more than twice – we started talking. He asked for my number and the rest was history. We began dating. After a while, I let him move in with me. Foolish, I know! I didn't tell you this...he didn't have his own place. He had been staying with his father and probably with one or two of his previous girlfriends as well. Now let me say this...all the time that I had been engaging in premarital sex (since age 14) and even in my first marriage, I never got pregnant. No STD's! Thank God, HIV hadn't come on the scene. He had three other children by two different women before me. I must have thought, pregnancy couldn't happen to me! But it did! I was okay with that. I had long since stopped attending church regularly because I knew my lifestyle and what I wanted to do was not matching up with what I knew in the Word of God. Remember, we were raised in the Word! For me, there was no point going to the church to hear what I already knew and I wasn't ready to give up the wrong for the right. Pregnant with my first child at 27 years-old with my live-in boyfriend! That's a blessing, right? Hmmm...(this saga to be continued).

Time for Reflections

How has your past impacted you, too, in the midst of looking for love in all the wrong places?

_____

_____

_____

_____

_____

_____

What costly lessons have you been forced to learn in the midst of failed relationships?

_____

_____

_____

_____

_____

_____

_____

Time for Reflections

If you have experienced a series of failed relationships, would it benefit you to seek advice or talk to a trusted friend or counselor? If so, have you begun this process? If not, what are you waiting on?

_____

_____

_____

_____

_____

_____

_____

Why do we seek love in ALL the wrong places instead of trusting the plan God has for us or waiting until He sends the person He has ordained for us to have?

_____

_____

_____

_____

_____

_____

_____

Time for Reflections

Even when we know that the relationship(s) we are in is an unhealthy one, what makes us want to stay in it instead of walking away?

_____

_____

_____

_____

_____

_____

_____

What are the warning signs that will confirm to you that he/she is 'not' the one?

_____

_____

_____

_____

_____

_____

_____

Time for Reflections

Can you identify a scripture passage that could have prevented you from going down this path had you taken the time to apply it to your life?

_____

_____

_____

_____

_____

_____

_____

_____

_____

_____

_____

_____

_____

_____

Chapter 5:
Discovering Me

> *"For I know the thoughts that I think toward you, saith the Lord, thoughts of peace, and not of evil, to give you an expected end. Then shall ye call upon Me, and ye shall go and pray unto Me, And I will hearken unto you. And ye shall seek Me, and find Me, When ye shall search for me with all your heart."*
> ### Jeremiah 29:11-13

After being in and out of multiple relationships and now pregnant at 27 with my very first child, I began to take life a little more seriously. I wanted to provide an excellent atmosphere for my child to be raised in. I purposed to eat the right foods. I even started going back to church.

As God would have it, I attended our church for a mid-week service. Our church was in revival that week. There was a man of God (can't remember now if he was a pastor or an evangelist). He was introduced as a cousin to singer, Diana Ross. During his message, conviction came over me so tough that on that night, I rededicated my life to the Lord! The values that I had been taught; the Word that had always been deposited on the inside of me down through the years, came totally alive on the inside of me. It was an evening I will never forget!

Note: Parents, stop fretting and spending sleepless nights over your children. Commit them (no matter what they are doing) to the Hands of their Creator ~ the All Wise and Sovereign God, our

Father ~ they (we) will make it back to Him! Why? Because that's the way God planned it! We are like sheep and the Good Shepherd won't allow us to stray too far outside of safe pasture. IF you have trained and raised them in the fear of the Lord, it will pay huge dividends on your behalf.

I returned home and shared the news with my live-in boyfriend ~ soon to be my baby's Daddy. Needless to say, that news wasn't received very well especially when it came time for me to tell him that he would have to move out. What?? Sandy, you mean you took that kind of stand the very first night of giving your life back to the Lord? Sure did! I told him I wanted to live my life for the Lord; that I wanted more from the Lord and I couldn't continue to live in sin. I told him I needed to be by myself. Naturally, I had to go through a few changes with him about that because he was in a comfort zone. But I knew what sin was and though I knew all along, it was the power of hearing the Word of God that would literally push me out of that situation.

Now, with no more than a few weeks into my pregnancy, I was ready to write a whole new chapter of my life. That one night at Emmanuel, I discovered me!

P.S. You will discover in later chapters that as quickly as I discovered myself in this particular season of my life, was almost as quick that I would lose myself again…going back to the familiar places. Don't skip pages though!

Time for Reflections

What is God's plan for your life? Can you feel it? Are you able to sense or discern it?

_____

_____

_____

_____

_____

_____

_____

 What happened in your life to cause you to have an epiphany… that "wake up" moment where you discovered who you really were?

_____

_____

_____

_____

_____

_____

_____

Time for Reflections

What worries or anxieties do you carry concerning your children and the paths they are currently on?

_____

_____

_____

_____

_____

Have you ever had an "enough is enough" moment in the midst of a relationship? What was it like for you?

_____

_____

_____

_____

_____

_____

Time for Reflections

If you were to write a story that expresses where you are in life right now, what would you name it? What would be the title that would best describe your present condition based on where you've been and what you've had to come through?

_____

_____

_____

_____

_____

_____

_____

_____

_____

_____

_____

_____

_____

Chapter 6: Discovering God

> "Ask, and it shall be given you; seek, and ye shall find; knock, and it shall be opened unto you: For everyone that asketh receiveth; and he that seeketh findeth; and to him that knocketh it shall be opened."
> **Matthew 7: 7-8**

Needless to say, while in the process of finding me, I also discovered GOD. I discovered that I really could hear and discern God's voice and that I was capable and willing to obey His instructions. Being willing to obey God is the crucial factor of our success in God! We are all capable of obeying God because of the power He has placed on the inside of those who have accepted Him as Lord. I also discovered that there was so much about Him and His Word that I knew, but had suppressed, because I wanted to live life on my own terms.

I discovered the depth of His Mercy and Love for a sinner like me! I discovered that He had never left nor turned His back on me…that it was me who had walked away from Him. Once I came to grips with all that seemed to be a life-changing revelation, my relationship with God was never the same.

I'm sure there were challenges that I may have faced preparing to live my life as a single mom, but to tell you quite honestly, I can't remember one! I had my own home and car; a job I loved and the peace of mind of knowing that it would just be me and my baby. No 'baby Daddy' drama; no trying to balance an ungodly relationship with carrying a child; no unnecessary stress levels. God had blessed me with an excellent family support system. He had kept me from bearing children for so long that all my family and friends were excited that my time for childbirth had finally come.

The Lord blessed me with incredible support during my pregnancy. My high school best friend was my unborn child's godmother, so she had already begun purchasing things for the baby. There was a young man I worked with who wanted to be my child's godfather, so he purchased the crib and helped me prepare the nursery room. Even as I was getting larger in my pregnancy, he would be there to support me; massage my back and shoulders, etc…just an excellent friend.

God blessed me to be given two baby showers with lots and lots of gifts. It was incredible to see how God would provide for me once I discovered that I had to put Him first.

June 16, 2010

I took a three month hiatus from writing this book because I just needed to rest. I was closing out my responsibilities working with a non-profit, and after that, I just wanted to relax my mind and spirit as well as close out some ministry projects that we had on our schedule.

But lo and behold, a lifelong friend, Mr. Clay Johnson, and I were in-boxing each other on Facebook. He had changed his profile picture which displayed his new book cover. Well, that was all I needed to see! I immediately sent an email to his publishing company and resumed writing. So if my thoughts seem to be broken up between these chapters (5 & 6), you will understand why.

Time for Reflections

Have there been times when you decided to really draw close to God and He proved Himself to you in ways you could have never imagined or thought possible? Explain.

_____

_____

_____

_____

_____

_____

_____

Just the mere act of obeying and surrendering our lives to the Lord brings about great blessings and rewards. Share your perspective on why it's been so hard for you to do just this very thing (obeying and surrendering your life fully to Him?) What is holding you back?

_____

_____

_____

_____

_____

_____

Chapter 7:
Every Time I Turn Around, I'm Back In Love Again!

"I know thy works, and thy labour, and thy patience, and how thou canst not bear them which are evil:.... Nevertheless I have somewhat against thee, because thou has left thy first love."
Revelation 2:2-4

Life with my newborn daughter was great! Kiana D'Nai Boyington was born on April 9, 1984. Let me go back a little. My pregnancy was great! I felt good; experienced no complications and totally stress-free during the actual pregnancy. However, when it came time to bring this baby forth, I experienced such pain as I had never known. I was taking a shower one night and I could feel my water had broken. After calling the doctor and everyone else, I went to the hospital to begin my labor process. Lord, help us women! And if Eve were around, she would get slapped by most of us, I'm sure!

I was in labor for 23 hours. The doctor came in and told me that the baby's head was too large to come through my birth canal. Oh, you don't say? You mean you couldn't have told me that like 10 hours ago? I had begun to develop toxemia and the baby was in distress. Doctors decided that I needed to be prepped for an emergency C-section which NO ONE had talked to me about at any time during my pregnancy! Needless to say, after all that trauma, God allowed me to bring forth a 9 lb. 13 oz. beautiful little girl.

Because I knew absolutely nothing about caring for a newborn, my best friend and my mom were with us around the clock when I brought Kiana home. I literally did nothing but rest and regain my physical strength while they both cared for my baby. I was so blessed! By the way, (to date) I still don't handle newborns!

I was a happy new mom! I would go to church with my baby and people would take her from me and keep her during the services, every Sunday. There was a young man who I had been in the church with all my life who had begun to take an interest in me. He was charming and handsome; suave and never at a loss for a compliment. He began wooing me and though I was quite satisfied as a single mom, the thought of this brother giving me and my baby so much attention was exciting for me. We started dating. He gave my baby so much love and attention and actually loved her as if she was his own. I refused to have much dealing with Kiana's natural father...I had actually moved past my past with that chapter in my life. Shelby Ray Crawford would pick us up for church and we would go to church as a family. He had a very loving and supportive family. Of course, my family absolutely loved him and thought he was the best thing on this side of "Kool-Aid".

When I took time to actually evaluate all of this, I realize that I fell in love with the love "Ray" had for me and especially for the love he had for Kiana. He offered us a life that wasn't without its baggage, but I knew he would try to move heaven and hell to please me. Ladies, what keeps us from loving a man who loves us to that degree? Why can't that be good enough? Why is it that when God sends us a Boaz, we always want one of Lucifer's angels? "Ray" and I were on the eve of being married when I finally opened my eyes long enough to admit that I didn't love him to the same extent he loved me. Though I should have been honest enough to tell him before we got married – even if it was the night before, I couldn't. So much work had gone into preparing for our wedding. His mom had been so generous in assisting us with all of our plans. Our families, friends and church family were so excited for us.

From the outside looking in, I had the best of all worlds. I didn't realize how much my past had affected me. I had gone on with life but I had never really dealt with it. "Ray" and I married and stayed together for two years. To date, we remain good friends. I love his current wife and their children call me "Auntie" and will always be grateful to Shelby Ray Crawford for sharing that part of my life. He was a refreshing breeze for a girl who had experienced more than I could have ever shared with him because he knew, loved and respected my family. Most of all, I am grateful that God sent Johnnie Ann to be his angel because he so deserved to enjoy a life and a love that I was incapable of giving. Because of God's incredible and merciful love, we are all amazingly close friends and have been there for each other during our most crucial trials. I am so grateful that our relationship as families is a "God-thing". You ask…Sandy, what did you do? I'm glad you asked. I fell for my 'knight in shining armor' who really didn't know my story! (As God would have it, I saw the Crawford family exactly two days after writing this chapter so I could forewarn them that they were a part of my story!)

Fast-forward my story to a couple of years down 'my' road…

While working, I used to notice this guy who would walk through the building. He would walk on my floor; say, "hello", give me a smile and would keep it moving. He did this several times during the course of the day, each day until (I guess) he got the nerve to strike up a conversation. I recall the first thing he said to me was about my personalized license plates on my car. He wanted to know what the initials meant. Then, he got around to asking if I was a happily married woman, and offering some small talk here and there. Some few weeks later, I was at the mall having photos taken of my daughter. It's ALWAYS my daughter!! (smile)

Talk about coincidence or happenstances…which by the way, I don't believe in at all! It is my belief that anything that happens in our lives – be it good or bad – happens for a reason and whatever the outcome, it serves as a lifelong teaching tool that you will remember down the road. Such has been the story of my life. Whether positive or negative the situation, God has used these experiences to teach me valuable lessons along my journey. *Romans 8:28 reads "And we know that all things work together for good to them that love God, to them who are the called according to His purpose."*

As life would have it, while at the photography studio that fateful (don't get it twisted…I didn't say 'faithful') evening, my new found male friend at work and a friend of his, were also at the shopping mall. He had stopped and watched as the photographer was taking the photos of me and Kiana and he, too, fell in love with my little girl. He held her and began to play with her. We talked briefly and he went on his way. That was innocent enough!

The very next day, this guy came to my office with a gift bag in his hand. He smiled and told me to open it up. I will never forget it. I pulled out a blue 2 piece Gucci outfit that he had purchased for my daughter after seeing us at the mall the night before. Did I fall in love with him right then? Naw! But I fell in love with his gesture. I thought it was pretty special for him to give me a gift for my little girl. Ladies, what's the way to a single mom's heart? I don't know about you, but for this single mom, it must have been the demonstration of care and special attention given to my child. For me, I believe it somewhat compensated for the absence of her biological father, who would have brought more drama to the father/child relationship than it was worth for me.

I don't remember much about how this relationship progressed after that particular day. It just seemed to take off after that. We talked more. He visited my office more. My boss and co-workers liked him. I don't even recall when we officially started a serious relationship…I just know that we did. Soon, we were spending time together every day. He loved taking me out to eat; going to the lake and enjoying the outdoors.

Darren was affiliated with a van club so we would go away on weekend trips with other members of the van club, and soon became known as a couple. One day out of the blue, his mom came knocking on my door and introduced herself to me. She said her son had told her about me so she wanted to meet the young lady who was spending so much time with her son. This should have been a red light right there, right? She was curious; asked a lot of questions and gave a little information that I never asked her for. I was never much of a talker with people I didn't know. She told me that she lived right around the corner…oh-kay!!!

Before long, every day evolved around our relationship. We could talk about anything. I believe our relationship became so special because we became friends first. We shared a lot about our pasts…past relationships, relationships with our families, having the workplace discussions in common, etc. As our relationship continued, Darren was actually the very person that I had ever shared the details of my childhood with. He took great interest in me being mixed with Asian descent. I partly believe that the major reason I felt at ease sharing the heartache of my past with him is, because he was the first person that I had been in relationship with who did not know my stepfather. My stepdad passed away during my marriage to Shelby Crawford.

Somehow I felt safe with Darren. He had a tender and compassionate heart and admitted that he had closer relationships with females than he did with males. Another red flag, huh? Not really for me, because I was the same way. We had so many characteristics that were the same. So much about our personalities was similar.

I shared my entire life with Darren. I could cry in his arms and he made me feel safe. He couldn't judge my stepdad because he never knew him. My stepdad's reputation as a Christian father and deacon of the church could not be tarnished because Darren had nothing to compare or contrast him to. Darren didn't judge my mother. He didn't treat my family any differently. So here I was…back in love again!!

Time for Reflections

Why do we tend to let the good ones go? What does that say about you?

_____

_____

_____

_____

_____

_____

 Have you tried to move on from your past without dealing with it? Do you realize how much that is hindering you? Explain.

_____

_____

_____

_____

_____

_____

Time for Reflections

What type of relationships did you move into before being healed or made whole from your past?

_____

_____

_____

_____

_____

_____

For me, satan always kept "men" as a snare and a hindrance to me. What is your snare? What seems to be your hindrance?

_____

_____

_____

_____

_____

_____

_____

Time for Reflections

In this chapter, I shared that I was incapable of fully giving myself in love to others because I had not received love early in my own life. Do you agree that we are incapable of giving what we haven't received? Explain.

_____

_____

_____

_____

_____

_____

They say that hurting people tend to go around hurting others. Why does that happen and how can you prevent or change this?

_____

_____

_____

_____

_____

_____

Chapter 8:
Getting Past
My Past

> *"Therefore also now, saith the Lord, turn ye even to me with all your heart, and with fasting, and with weeping, and with mourning: And rend your heart, and not your garments, and turn unto the Lord your God: for He is gracious and merciful, slow to anger, and of great kindness, and repenteth Him of the evil. Who knoweth if He will return and repent, and leave a blessing behind Him; even a meat offering and a drink offering unto the Lord your God?* Joel 2:12-14

Actually, my relationship with Darren helped to heal many of the hurts from my past. Because I had kept all of these secrets bottled up for so long, having the ability or freedom to release it all was life-changing for me. I no longer felt the need to hide anything.

After being free to share my past with Darren, I found myself later being able to share my past in ministry. I was asked to minister my first message. The ministry that God has given to me is to be transparent with those I minister to. In my message, the Holy Spirit unctioned me to share my story. The theme for those of us who were scheduled to minister was "But God!" It was taken from the story of Joseph in Genesis 38. As I began to minister about the life of Joseph and how God used all his trials; all of his obstacles and all of his difficulties; how his enemies – even those in his own household – turned their backs on him and tried to destroy him, his *'But God'* moment blessed me and strengthened me to boldly share my own 'But God' moments! Many as they were, I know if it had not been for the love and favor of God upon my life, I could not have stood as Joseph did to declare "what the enemy meant for evil in my life, God had turned it for good!" That became my story and I am sticking to it!!

After preaching that first message, I felt incredible freedom. Though I didn't know what my fellow church members would think about me, that really didn't matter. I knew I had obeyed God. After the service, people came to me in tears to share similar stories and how my message blessed them to know that someone had made it pass their past!

This season in my life freed me to confront my past; release it and now my only purpose for looking back on it would be to share my testimony with others! I could forgive my mom; I had forgiven my stepdad and had even forgiven myself! I knew God was bringing forth healing. I knew God was doing a new thing in me! I could feel burdens being lifted. And most importantly, I knew my story was a key to others being healed from their pasts as well! Getting past my past was refreshing!

Time for Reflections

Consider your "but God" moment (s). With all that satan has put in your way to destroy you, how has God intervened on your behalf?

_____

_____

_____

_____

_____

_____

_____

What steps have you taken to get past your past?

_____

_____

_____

_____

_____

_____

Time for Reflections

Are you free to share your story? Explain.

_____

_____

_____

_____

_____

_____

_____

_____

_____

_____

_____

_____

_____

_____

_____

_____

Chapter 9:
The Process

This is probably the longest chapter…

Definition of "'Process'": a continuing development, involving many changes.

Time with Darren turned into years. We were together for 4 years before we got married. This part of my life could actually be the basis of another book!! Maybe I could entitle it, "Heartache & Pain, Sunshine & Rain!"

As I had mentioned in a previous chapter, Darren had admitted to me that he shared closer relationships with females than he did with males. To put it lightly, that was a gross understatement! To my disappointment, this man to whom I had given my heart to completely, would be the same man who would crush it a thousand times over. As I've heard in a movie whose title escapes me now, our marriage was both the best of times and the worst of times.

I need to go back a couple of years to let you know that all that I had discovered about me and then about God as mentioned in chapters 5 and 6, took a back seat in the midst of my growing relationship with Darren Jackson. In the 4 years before we married, I fornicated with him (just in case you naively say you don't know what that means…I engaged in ongoing and consistent sexual activity without the benefit of marriage, for all of those years). Enjoying the sexual relationship made it easier for us to decide to "shack up" or cohabit the same living quarters.

After all, if you are going to choose to sin against God and be guilty of turning your back on the very One who had rescued, healed and delivered you, you somehow convince yourself that you might as well go all the way, huh?!

The bad thing and, for me, would have been the most dangerous thing if God had ended my life, was that I was a Sunday School teacher. I also sang and served as President of the church choir. I began teaching Sunday School while I was married to Shelby Crawford. I was blessed to have a thriving young Adult Sunday School class, striving to live their lives for God. Here I was, their biblical teacher, teaching them one thing, while living quite another. Because God had already 'anointed' me with a transparent ministry, it was my duty to share with my class the double life I was guilty of leading. There were many days, through my own study and prayer time, that I was convicted enough to ask God to forgive me but not convicted enough to repent (actually be godly sorry and then to turn away from the sin).

I would go to church and teach others, encouraging the class members not to find themselves caught up in the mess that I was in! I found myself telling them how easy it is to fall back into a sinful state, all while thinking you are strong enough to not get put back in the devil's trap! I was honest with them and honest with Darren. The weight of sin was horrible for me. I knew I had put my relationship with this man before my relationship with God…and I knew better. I realized that I had chosen Darren over the relationship I discovered, and came to treasure, with my God! Still, my love and desire to be with Darren was going to cost my relationship with God and seemingly, from my continued actions, I didn't care. If you could judge me by my actions (because I didn't immediately give it up), you wouldn't know that I was being convicted of my sin.

I finally talked with my Pastor and also to two of my fellow Sunday School teachers. I had finally come to the point that I decided to stop teaching one thing and then living another.

I told them that I was going to give up my Sunday School class and stop teaching because I was living in sin. Now think about what I said and what I was prepared to do... Here I was ready to give up the very thing that God had anointed, gifted, called and ordained for me to do all because I wasn't ready to give up the pleasures of sin. I had made the decision that it was more important to me to continue a life of sin, all while being well aware of the consequences *("the wages of sin is death........Romans 6:23a)* than to make the choice to give up my life of sin and do things God's way. Call me crazy or what? Actually, I had allowed the pleasures of sin to blind me! I would try to chalk it up to me having a case of spiritual amnesia, but God told me that excuse wouldn't fly. I knew the truth of God's Word...after all, I taught it! I knew that I was headed for hell while teaching others how to live in victory. I was double-minded, that's what I was. I forsook my relationship with my God and jeopardized my salvation. How much sense does that make for someone who is calling themselves a Christian?

As I mentioned, I met with my fellow Sunday School teachers to tell them I was going to stop teaching. I told them I wasn't living what I was teaching and didn't feel worthy to continue teaching. I thought they would both agree with my position. Much to my surprise, they both strongly encouraged me not to stop teaching. What they spoke into my life was invaluable and something that I will never forget. It is also the reason that we need accountability partners in ministry. These two Sunday School teachers told me that if I decided to stop doing the very thing that God had gifted me to do, I would prolong my own deliverance. If I stopped teaching, I would be content with sin because I wouldn't be motivated to stay in the Word of God. As long as I kept teaching, my spirit would be open to hear God. What I was teaching would bring conviction and allow God to have His way in me. In tears, I received the words they spoke into my spirit. They encouraged me and prayed with me. From that day forward, I never looked at a Christian's journey the same way. I always believed that if you were living a life of sin while serving in the church, you should be required to sit down. I always believed that while 'they' shouldn't be put out of the church, sinning or carnal Christians should not knowingly be allowed to preach/teach one thing and then live another. I always believed that this "straddling the fence" lifestyle weakens the church and the Body of Christ because it allowed other believers to think that two-faced lifestyle as a Christian was acceptable to God and the church. Let me affirm this...it is not acceptable! God does not accept sin in any form among those who say we have accepted Him as Lord in our lives. I just saw things rigidly until I had to live it out for myself. Through my own sin lifestyle, I saw that oftentimes coming or choosing to come out of sin is a process. Such a struggle between our flesh and spirit takes place and based on which part of our being we choose to give ear to the most, will be the part which gets the victory!

I went home and shared the outcome of my meeting with Darren. He also knew the struggle I was experiencing. He had never professed a hope in Christ. His family was raised as Jehovah Witnesses. I knew my consent to sin with him would also serve to hinder him ever making a decision to accept Christ.

Though I can't tell you exactly when and don't really recall the vivid details, one day I decided that enough was enough. Darren and I had discussed marriage but it was only because I knew my spiritual dilemma. He didn't want me miserable knowing I was trying to live for God. It was never that he really wanted marriage at the time. He had been married before as well. One day, I came home and told him that I just couldn't do this anymore. It came seemingly out of nowhere for Darren because overall, we enjoyed a good "sinful" life together, shacking up. Our only obstacles – which I'll talk more about later – were other women...his other women!

Finally, full conviction came. Finally, I was ready to do things God's way. Finally, I was ready to say "yes" to God and say "no" to Darren. Strength seemingly came out of nowhere, but God had been moving by His Spirit the entire time. He was just allowing me time to choose whether I wanted to live or die. I told

Darren that I could no longer live with him without being married. He had just purchased a duplex home that we shared with his mom living on one side and us on another. I told him I loved him, but I loved God more. I told him if we couldn't be married, I would have to move. Though he didn't want me to move, he wasn't willing to get married right then. He had fallen in love with my daughter and we had begun to build a successful life together. I knew he didn't want to marry, so I made it easy for him and me. That same day, I began packing and preparing to move. I moved with my mom until I could find an apartment. It was like a weight lifted. I felt free and I felt good. I knew I would have to still see Darren at work every day but I was prepared to handle that. It was like a light bulb went off one day asking me "why did it take you so long?"

> *"For we know that the law is spiritual: but I am carnal, sold under sin. For that which I do, I allow not: for what I would, that do I not; but what I hate, that do I...for I know that in me (that is, in my flesh,) dwelleth no good thing...O wretched man that I am!)*
> ***Romans 7:14-15, 18 & 24.***

Time for Reflections

What did this chapter speak to you?

_____

_____

_____

_____

_____

_____

Describe a time when you were caught between what God says and what you knew vs. what your flesh wanted to do?

_____

_____

_____

_____

_____

_____

Time for Reflections

What is the price you have had to pay for failing to obey God when you knew better?

_____

_____

_____

_____

_____

How can someone who is living in sin (practicing a sin lifestyle) YET going to church every Sunday be transformed and become sold out for Christ?

_____

_____

_____

_____

_____

_____

Time for Reflections

Why do we take so long to decide to do the right thing?

_____

_____

_____

_____

_____

_____

What do you see as your role and responsibility to assist carnal Christians or the unsaved to encourage them to change their behaviors?

_____

_____

_____

_____

_____

_____

_____

Time for Reflections

I shared that I was in church – teaching; singing in the choir and serving in the church but would have bust hell wide open while living a sin lifestyle. What about you? What does your current lifestyle reflect?

_____

_____

_____

_____

_____

_____

_____

_____

_____

_____

_____

_____

_____

_____

Chapter 10: My Misery Birthed My Ministry

> *"But as for you, ye thought evil against me, but God meant it unto good, to bring to pass, as it is this day, to save much people alive."* **Genesis 50:20**

Finally, and after the process, I celebrated my emancipation! After living with someone for 4 years and playing the role of a wife without a marriage license (or any other marital benefits), I was free! Or so I thought…

I had this bright idea! Since I was free and out of a day to day relationship, I decided to schedule a doctor's appointment. I wanted to make sure there were no communicable diseases; just wanted to make sure I was medically sound to begin a new life. Nothing had prepared me for this chapter in my life! I went to the doctor; had all my tests ran – pap smear, urine, everything! The medical office told me to call in two days for my lab results on everything. No big deal! Or so I thought…

I remember this like it was yesterday. One day in the year 1990, I was sitting in my office at work. I called the medical office to get my results as they had instructed.

The medical assistant pulled my records and came back to the phone saying "Congratulations, your test results came back positive!"

Me: "Positive? What? What test results?"
Medical Assistant: "Your urine test! You are going to have a

baby!"

Me: "What? Me? Are you sure you don't have the wrong file? It couldn't be me!! (Stupid…as if I hadn't been having sex!)

Medical Assistant (pausing): "Yes, it's you! We need to get you set up for your prenatal visits!"

Everything after that was a total blank!! I hung up the phone and cried my heart out! How could this happen? Now? Not at this time! Not when I had finally mustered up enough strength and courage to tell God "yes"! NO! This just could not be happening to me!! And certainly not after I decided to finally obey God and stop living in sin!! I was no more good!

I remember going home crying to my mom telling her that I didn't want to tell Darren. When we were living together, he would say all the time that he wanted me to have his baby. He would say he wanted us to have our love child. But for me…not now! My mom convinced me to tell him…or come to think about it, she may have told him. I just really don't remember. I do remember that he wanted to take me out so we went to "Houston's" to talk about it. He asked me what I wanted to do. He knew I hadn't set out to trap him with a baby. He could see how terribly devastated I was. I honestly don't even remember how the rest of the evening went.

I may have entered into the twilight zone, because days and weeks passed by. Then one day while at work, little things started happening. Darren had called my office and left a message for me. A few other incidentals took place at work, but nothing special caught my attention. Then, he called and asked me to meet him over at the med school which was where we would go take our breaks during the day to just sit and talk. I can say that Darren and I became good friends during our relationship. We could always talk with each other. When I got over to the med school, he was already there waiting. He asked me about my day. He also asked me about the phone message he had left for me and the other incidentals. I, being totally naïve, was totally in the dark. I remember feeling frustrated because it seemed like he was trying to play mind games with me. I had too much stuff on my mind to play guessing games with Darren! After he began sorting the phone message out and the other incidentals, it became a message that he had hoped I would have understood. The message and the 'incidentals' that occurred summed up the message that read "Will you marry me?" Oh, you talk about crocodile tears! He held me and told me that he loved me and that he would not have me going through this pregnancy alone. Ok, ladies…can you guess what my answer was? You got it…a teary, unequivocal, "yes"!

We went back to work and he showed all my co-workers his message. Come to find out, they knew what he was going to do and helped him pull it together. When I got back to my office, the Lord spoke to me ever so clearly. "See, My child, I told you I would give you the desires of your heart. I just needed to see if you would put Me first before I could give it to you!" Tears, tears and more tears followed the remainder of that day. I also knew in my heart that though Darren wasn't truly ready for marriage, he loved and respected me enough to not have me carry his child without being married. I knew that!

Thus, in February, 1991, I became Mrs. Darren Jackson. For the 10 years we were married, it was like we had a dual life. A Dr. Jekyll and Mr. Hyde, if you will. When my husband was at home and with our family, life was good. He was a hard-working man. An excellent provider. A wonderful stepfather to Kiana. He loved to cook and grill for us. He thrived on family vacations and outings. He loved seeing our children romp around playing and discovering life. He loved his secluded "cave" time in his den. He loved the life we lived as husband and wife as the Jackson family. Yet, there was a part of him that could not be content with a settled family life. My husband had an insatiable appetite for women. You couldn't determine if he had a certain protocol for those he would select because I don't think it really mattered much. He had black women; white women; Asian women; skinny women; fat women; attractive women and downright, unattractive women. It would be years into our marriage and even after being separated and then later reconciled, that God would give me a revelation concerning Darren. The revelation finally released me from the bitterness and unforgiveness I felt towards him. Now I loved me some Darren Jackson! All in all, he was just easy to love. He was attentive; generous; we could talk about most things and we enjoyed our time together. He was the very first man that I shared my childhood with. The revelation that God gave me was that Darren's need (or desires) for other women was a generational curse that he had come up under. For him, most of the relationships began innocent enough, just as it did with me...as fellow co-workers or discovering that they shared things in common. After getting to know these ladies and them confiding in him, my husband simply (and sickly) felt that he was the solution to these females' problems. He made every effort to be that – to the demise of our marriage.

Ladies, I don't know if you've ever loved your husband so much that you prayed and cried; cried and prayed, daily asking God to change things. Yet, no matter how much you prayed or how badly you cried, God didn't seem to be listening!

In the midst of our marriage, my Pastor had come and asked me to serve as the Marriage Ministry leader of our church. Surely, she must have been on drugs! She must have lost her anointing! She definitely could not have heard from the Lord on this one! Me...the woman whose husband did not attend church. Me...the one who was into her third marriage, and even this one wasn't working out! Me...the one who could not maintain a strong and successful marital relationship! Before telling her "no", I had to ask her why she would even consider me as a leader in Marriage Ministry. Certainly, I wasn't qualified for this. My own marriage wasn't succeeding – and no other marriage before this one succeeded. Let me pause right here. How many times have we heard someone say "If you haven't succeeded in (whatever it is...could be marriage, finances, parenting, ministry, etc.), how can you tell me how to do something when you couldn't do it? How many times have you said or heard others say all too often "How can a broke person teach me how to be rich?" The answer is, you'd be surprised! Let me share this nugget with you. Be extremely careful how you turn someone off that is going (or has gone) through. Just because they experienced failure or disappointment in their own situations, does not disqualify them for ministry or service to you. Peter denied Christ – not once – but three times, so how was he later 'qualified' to stand and cause the onset of the early church? Paul condemned and persecuted Christians. How in the world could he be 'qualified' to begin and continue a mass movement for thousands to come to know Christ?

All of our testimonies can lead to birthing something awesome in our lives. In my case, my misery birthed my ministry. And it was discovered that my ministry was not merely to married couples, but to those who had experienced childhood abuse. But not only to the abused, but to the rejected or to those who felt unloved and taken for granted. My misery birthed my ministry, because I didn't want to see Christian marriages fail. You see, my husband did not share the same love that I did for Christ. So for me to see a husband and wife in church together every Sunday, demonstrated a hope and a passion in me to see Christian marriages stand, in spite of all the opposition. These marriages had something I didn't have in mine and I was determined to openly share both the things I had learned and my experiences in order to save a marriage, even though mine was crumbling. It was as if the demise of my own marriage served as fuel to light a fire in me to not see others go through what I was going through. I came to understand that my determination to take care of God's business, while trusting Him to take care of mine, would open the door for God to handle my stuff and set me up for my own rewards!

Time for Reflections

How has God taken the pain of your past to cause it to work for your good?

_____

_____

_____

_____

_____

_____

Can you attest to this statement concerning your past…"it wasn't easy but it was worth it?" Explain.

_____

_____

_____

_____

_____

_____

_____

Time for Reflections

Have you ever really loved someone so much yet everything in you said to release them and let them go? Share how this made you feel.

_____

_____

_____

_____

_____

_____

_____

In the midst of your misery, what level of ministry are you sensing God wants to birth in and through you?

_____

_____

_____

_____

_____

_____

_____

Time for Reflections

With all that you have experienced, who are the people that you know you can reach? Who are the folks that God has released you to bless and encourage just by sharing your story?

_____

_____

_____

_____

_____

_____

_____

What instances in your life have caused you to question if God really cared about what you were going through?

_____

_____

_____

_____

_____

_____

_____

Chapter 11:
A Woman On A Mission

"For thus saith the Lord, That after seventy years be accomplished at Babylon, I will visit you, and perform My good Word toward you, in causing you to return to this place. For I know the thoughts that I think toward you, saith the Lord, thoughts of peace, and not of evil, to give you an expected end. Then shall ye call upon Me, and ye shall go and pray unto Me, and I will hearken unto you. And ye shall seek Me, and find Me, when ye shall search for Me with all your heart. And I will be found of you, saith the Lord: and I will turn away your captivity, and I will gather you from all the nations, and from all the places whither I have driven you, saith the Lord; and I will bring you again into the place whence I caused you to be carried away captive." **Jeremiah 29:10-14**

At the time of this writing, we are in Branson, Missouri. It is December, 2010 and we are here to celebrate my husband's birthday. It seems that I can only focus on my book when we steal away from the hustle and bustle of everyday life. (Even now, it is September, 2011 and we are in Branson again as I continue to type my manuscript). My thoughts seem to come together (as a ready writer) and I begin to easily flow when God allows me to steal away and find rest. I am determined to have finished (at least the writing of) this book before the year ends.

God gave me revelation of Jeremiah 29:10-14 while attending a special service where a friend of our family was giving her initial sermon. As long as I have been reading the Bible, I honestly don't think I had heard this particular passage of scripture, until that night. The Lord used this young lady in an awesome way to share the truth of His Word found in Jeremiah. She began to share her own personal story of struggles, indecision, pain, rejection, and hurt – you know all that stuff that lies inside of us that many of us don't want to talk about; let alone, share it publicly with others. It is unfortunate that the Body of Christ feels that we cannot be transparent. It is sad that we try to masquerade our faces with fake smiles, knowing that we are dying on the inside. But bless God! This young minister of the Gospel shared how God was using her misery to birth her ministry. After hearing and reading Jeremiah 29:10-14, I was able to look at my own life differently. No matter what I was experiencing...no matter how my heart was hurting, God was reassuring me that He knew the plans He thought toward me! It was overwhelming for me to know that in the midst of all my pain and disappointment, that my God really did have plans for peace and not evil; plans for good and not bad in my life; to give me a hope and an expected end!! His end would be one that would enrich and bless my life – not destroy it! It may seem a small thing to you, but once I came into that truth, I became a woman on a mission!

It was like a literal 'jump start' had been given to me on that night. Let me pause here...I caution you to never sell someone short who is ministering the Gospel. It may not come in the usual manner in which you are accustomed. It may not come by the man or woman of God that you are usually used to hearing and receiving from. The Gospel message that can and will change your entire life may come from one you would least expect. Remember, God uses the foolish things of this world to confound the wise.

This young woman of God had experienced much transition. She had fought demons after demons who warred with her to prevent her from fulfilling her call and reaching her destiny. Satan has the same trap set for me and you. His thinking is that if he can keep us beat down in depression, self-doubt, insecurity, pain, rejection, betrayal, disappointments from our past and all those other devices, you and I will be too despondent or depressed to do and be what God has for us. I am grateful to God that more and more, the Holy Spirit is showing us that God can work wonders with a mess!

I left that service to never be the same. I had an unquenchable desire to be about my Father's business. If the Lord would show me a need, I was determined to see what I could do to help meet the need. God gave me a heart for hurting people. When God showed me pain, heartache or devastation, I was quickly moved by the Holy Spirit to minister; to pray and to encourage. God began to show me the ministry of encouragement. He had placed upon me a mantle in the Barnabas ministry. *Acts 13-15* Barnabas was a co-laborer and partner of the Apostle Paul. He traveled with him to encourage people to hear and receive God's message of hope, healing, deliverance, salvation and restoration.

I didn't see myself as a talker, and definitely, not an orator or preacher. Sometimes, I could see a spirit of hurt on someone and the Lord would just move me to go hold them…not talk; not orally minister but to just hold and embrace them in their pain. It was at that moment that God would allow me to feel the pain and that He would show me how to pray for the individual.

Here I was a broken woman from her childhood to her third marriage. I was a woman who was broken as a child. I was a woman who had not been healed as a child, but was becoming a teen. I was a woman who walked through her teen years still looking for love in all the wrong places because I had not been healed as a child. I had become a woman in and out of multiple relationships because I had been seeking to love and be loved ever since I was a child.

Then Jeremiah 29:10-14 was presented to me! I finally understood that everything I had experienced throughout my own life would be used to liberate and set the captives free! This passage of scripture pushed me to become a woman on a mission!

The mission was to encourage men and women; boys and girls to let them know that there was nothing so devastating that had occurred in their lives that God could not handle. There was no pain or disappointment that God could not heal. That no matter who came; who left; who hurt you; who betrayed you; who stole from you; who cheated on you…God could take all of that and use you for a mighty work in the earth. All of our tests could become our greatest testimony!

God had opened up my mouth and my heart and showed me that I didn't have to be fearful or feel ashamed of all the things I had gone through. And although some - maybe most of them – could have been prevented, they were all necessary and expedient for me to experience because of the calling God had placed on my life! Yes, a woman on a mission! Ready to share my life with others as an open book so girls wouldn't have to experience the same hurts I felt. A woman on a mission to speak into the lives of young ladies that everything they are searching for in a *human* man can only truly be fulfilled through the GOD man who would love them in a way no *human* man ever could! A woman on a mission that could speak into the lives of other couples to encourage them not to go through the things I had experienced.

The birthing of my ministry was conceived in pain! The seeds that God would use to put me in a call to ministry were seeds of abuse; mistrust; disappointment; heartache; lack of self-worth and lack of understanding – yet, these very seeds have produced a wonderful harvest on God's behalf as others have been ministered to, counseled, strengthened and encouraged. God proved to me that He certainly knew the thoughts that He was thinking towards me…things I didn't see; things I never could have seen; things I would have never thought possible, but by the

Grace of an All-Wise, All Knowing and Loving Father!! This is what God did on my behalf….after the years of captivity; after all the years of being held in bondage – God moved and set me free! A woman on a mission – could that now be YOU?

Time for Reflections

What did this particular chapter minister to you?

_____

_____

_____

_____

_____

_____

Through all of my pain; through all of my disappointments, God did a work in me. Through it all, I became a woman on a mission...how about you?

_____

_____

_____

_____

_____

_____

_____

Time for Reflections

Identify a biblical passage that speaks to you after reading this chapter.

_____

_____

_____

_____

_____

_____

_____

_____

_____

_____

_____

_____

_____

_____

Chapter 12: There Is A Story Behind My Praise!

"Be glad then, ye children of Zion, and rejoice in the Lord your God: for He hath given you the former rain moderately, and He will cause to come down for you the rain, the former rain, and the latter rain in the first month. And the floors shall be full of wheat, and the vats shall overflow with wine and oil. And I will restore to you the years that the locust hath eaten, the cankerworm, and the caterpillar, and the palmerworm, my great army which I sent among you." Joel 2:23-25

It is my sincere prayer that you have been blessed by reading this book about my life. As you can readily see, God created and then fashioned me into a woman who would one day preach the Gospel. But before He would fashion me, He loved me through "all the junk in my trunk"...the emotional baggage and bondage...the hurt and pain from childhood through adulthood...all the scars and all the scares, God was there all the time!!

Before I could be given a mission, there would be things I had to miss! With all that I experienced and all that I had to endure, God kept me! I could have lost my mind, but He kept me! I could have given up all hope in life, but God rescued me! My life could have been empty, pitiful and sad, but God sheltered me in the midst of it all.

I stand before you now to speak into your life. I need to tell you that God is able! I need you to know that with all the pain, disappointment and heartache, God still gives you a reason to praise! Look at your life. Consider all the things you've gone through…everything you've endured. I know it's easy to say it shouldn't have had to be this way. Life should have been much different. Do you know what I've come to know? That in the midst of all the bad stuff; in the midst of all the negativity; in the midst of everything satan does (or has done) to try to destroy me, I am still here! Still standing! And stronger than I ever thought I could be!

As I look back over my life, I realize that in the midst of all that mess, I am stronger! In the midst of all the pain, I'm better! In the midst of all that I suffered, I made it to the other side of 'through'! I declare to you this day, **IN JESUS' NAME**, that you will, too!

I look at my life now and from the outside looking in, it appears that there are no traces of my painful past. Yet, whenever I go to a movie that tells a story anything similar to what I experienced, I can feel the sting of my past all over again. Not that it haunts me, but it's there as a reminder of all that I have been through. When people see me in communion with God, and the tears of joy and thanksgiving flow ever so freely, it is a testimony of how good God has been to me! I not only have lived long enough to share my story, but I thrive on sharing it because I know how much it will bless others. My past is a painful story for my family. It is a grave reminder of the worst of times in what appeared to so many others, that it should have been the best of times!

Now, I have peace that surpasses all of my understanding. In a message entitled, "God Can Turn Back Time", Joel Osteen stated that "the depth of your past is an indication of the height of your future!" That message had an astounding impact on me. My past was traumatic! My past was unfair! My past caused me to make some choices that affected my latter years. I recognize that I am healed and walking in my deliverance every day. I understand that my life has been an amazing journey in, first, discovering who I am but most importantly, discovering just how much God loves me. Through the eyes of my past, I have come to know that the Lord will go to amazing lengths to turn our past into our praise!

I am grateful because I have been blessed to have lived long enough to be able to declare to you this day that "There Is A Story Behind My Praise!" When the tears fall, it is because I know I have so much to thank God for! When I go forth in ministry, it is because I know that God is truly real! When I testify so boldly about His goodness, it is because I realize just how good He's been to me! Through all that I have had to come through, I can declare unto the highest mountain, that "**There Is A Story Behind My Praise**!"

The Writing Of My Manuscript Finally Completed On March 18, 2011 In Branson, Missouri.
The Actual Typing Of My Manuscript Finally Completed On September 5, 2011 In Branson, Missouri.

And Yes, There Is (Truly) A Story Behind My Praise!!

Time for Reflections

I have shared my story. You have your story. With all that you have gone through, how has God proven Himself to be real to you?

_____

_____

_____

_____

_____

_____

As you reflect on your life story, where do you see God taking you from here? And what steps will you need to take to get there?

_____

_____

_____

_____

_____

_____

Time for Reflections

How have you determined to truly move past your own past?

_____

_____

_____

_____

_____

_____

How can you now be bold enough to share your testimony and seek to encourage others who have walked in your shoes?

_____

_____

_____

_____

_____

_____

_____

Time for Reflections

How has reading this book enabled you to see to what lengths satan wants to destroy you but how God has interceded and blocked the plan of the enemy in your life?

_____

_____

_____

_____

_____

_____

As you close the book, you know that whatever happened in your life, you see you are still here! The situation(s) didn't take you out! Your past didn't kill you! You have survived! Where will you go from here to tell the world that you, too, have "a story behind YOUR praise?"

_____

_____

_____

_____

_____

_____

Time for Reflections

Time for Reflections

Testimonials:

Prophetess & Evangelist Earlene Davis:

I have read the book, "There Is A Story Behind My Praise", written by my daughter, Pastor Cassandra Wainright. This book expresses heartache and sorrow that she experienced growing up as a young girl living in our home. Sadly, we were all experiencing the heartache, sorrow and madness that no family should ever have to go through.

Believe me, as you read this story, you would have had to go through this in order for you to truly understand and feel the pain. Both the love and heartache this child and her family endured…only God brought them through this with a sane mind to love and forgive as "our Lord has forgiven us!" To God Be The Glory!

P.S. I would have to say that God allowed her and our family to go through this to take us to the place we are today in Him! Trust God!!

LaTanya D. Cooper - Minister
Arlington, Texas :

I have known Cassandra Wainright for over 30 years. During this time, she has been a wife, mother, daughter, sister, aunt, goddaughter, ministry leader, pastor, community advocate, administrator extraordinaire and the list goes on! During this time, "I" have known her as a friend and a foe :), sister and sister-in-law :), partner-in-crime and partner-in-ministry :) and now I am proud to say that I know her as an AUTHOR!!!

Cassandra's, (or Sandy as she is known to most) book, "There Is A Story Behind My Praise", is a transparent look into her life and a testament to the forgiving, healing and transforming power of God. Sandy's story is one that her family and friends believe should have been told years ago! However, God's timing is perfect and the generation that needs to read it is now! Sandy shares the TRUTH, whether good, bad or ugly. I know the heart of Sandy Wainright and the ONLY reason that this book has been birthed is for the glory of God and the deliverance of man.

My prayer is that God will lead Sandy to the RIGHT people in the RIGHT places to guide and assist her in getting this word to the nations.

Are there other books that address these issues already out there? Of course there are, but none are as open, as transparent and as honest as Sandy's!!!

Sandy is a diamond in the rough and I pray God's ridiculous blessings upon her and this work!!!

There Is A Story Behind My Praise

As Sung By: Carolyn Traylor

There's a story behind my praise
That's why my hands I'll continue to raise!
I'm gonna praise Him for the rest of my days,
Oh, there's a story behind my praise!

There's a story behind my praise
That's why my hands I'll continue to raise!
I'm gonna praise Him for the rest of my days,
Oh, there's a story behind my praise!

If you see me crying, that is a story
How He's been God for me in all of His Glory!
If you see me shouting, oh, don't be amazed...
I just realized where and when I was saved!!

When you see me running, oh, don't you think it strange!
My whole life, He's rearranged!
There is a story behind my praise, my praise, my praise!
There is a story behind my praise!

There's a real long story; I can't tell it all!
But when I think of how He brought me out!
There is a story behind my praise!
There is a story ~ how He allowed me to keep my mind,
There is a story behind my praise!!

I love You, GOD!
Yeah, there is a story behind my praise!

About The Author

Cassandra Jackson-Wainright is a Friend of God. She serves as Pastor alongside her husband, Calvin C. Wainright, of Heaven Sent Outreach Ministries. She is also a teacher, encourager, intercessor, motivator and friend.

Cassandra is the second eldest daughter of a God fearing mother who taught and trained her in the Lord; the mother of two birth children; one God given daughter who has been an endless joy; two God-given sons from a blended union; and grandmother of her little sweethearts, Aa'Laiza Cole and Bailey Adams.